Constitution Day

Maeve Griffin

Real Life readers™

Rosen Classroom™

New York

Published in 2009 by The Rosen Publishing Group, Inc.
29 East 21st Street, New York, NY 10010

Copyright © 2009 by The Rosen Publishing Group, Inc.

All rights reserved. No part of this book may be reproduced in any form without permission in writing from the publisher, except by a reviewer.

Book Design: Michael J. Flynn

Photo Credits: Cover © JustASC/Shutterstock; pp. 3 (background), 4–5 (background), 6–7 (background), 8 (background),11 (background), 12–13 (background), 15 (background), 16–17 (background), 19 (background), 20 (background), 22–23 (background), 24 (background) © Falko Matte/Shutterstock; p. 5 (students) © Monkey Business Images/Shutterstock; p. 6 (James Madison) © MPI/Hulton Archive/Getty Images; p. 9 © Stephen Coburn/Shutterstock; p. 10 (White House) © James Stidl/Shutterstock; p. 10 (Capitol) © Cristina Ciochina/Shutterstock; p. 10 (Supreme Court) © Jonathan Larsen/Shutterstock; p. 13 © MPI/Hulton Archive/Getty Images; p. 14 © APA/Hulton Archive/Getty Images; p. 17 (Robert Byrd) http://upload.wikimedia.org/wikipedia/commons/8/8e/Robert_Byrd_official_portrait.jpg; p. 17 (Harry Truman) http://upload.wikimedia.org/wikipedia/commons/9/92/Harry-truman.jpg; p. 18 © Michael Smith/Getty Images; p. 21 © Damir Karan/Shutterstock.

Library of Congress Cataloging-in-Publication Data

Griffin, Maeve.
  Constitution Day / Maeve Griffin.
     p. cm. - (Real life readers)
  Includes index.
  ISBN: 978-1-4358-0139-4
  6-pack ISBN: 978-1-4358-0140-0
  ISBN 978-1-4358-2978-7 (library binding)
  1. Constitution Day (U.S.)—Juvenile literature. 2. United States. Constitution—Anniversaries, etc.—Juvenile literature. 3. United States—Politics and government—1783-1789—Juvenile literature. 4. Constitutional history—United States—Juvenile literature. I. Title.
  E303.G75 2009
  320.973-dc22

2008036701

Manufactured in the United States of America

Contents

Honoring the Constitution … 4

The Constitutional Convention … 7

The Parts of the U.S. Constitution … 8

The Bill of Rights … 15

Why Do We Have Constitution Day? … 16

Ways to Celebrate Constitution Day … 19

Glossary … 23

Index … 24

Honoring the Constitution

Countries of the world are alike in many ways. Most countries have large cities. Many have lakes, rivers, forests, and plains. Some countries are covered with both sandy deserts and snowy mountains. The people who live in different countries may **celebrate** the same holidays and eat the same food, too.

However, countries always differ from each other in at least one way. All countries have their own laws and government. The U.S. **Constitution** describes how U.S. government works as well as the rights of U.S. citizens. The Constitution makes the United States a country unlike any other country. We celebrate Constitution Day each year on September 17. Let's find out how the Constitution was created and why it's honored with a special day.

Many schools use Constitution Day as a special day to learn about the U.S. Constitution.

6

The Constitutional Convention

In 1787, the United States was a young country. Several years before, the American colonies fought their British rulers and won their freedom. Each colony became a state with its own constitution. The **Articles of Confederation** shaped a central U.S. government. However, this government was too weak to make the thirteen states work together as one country.

In May 1787, leaders from each state except Rhode Island gathered in Philadelphia, Pennsylvania, to form a stronger central government. This meeting, called the Constitutional **Convention**, took place in the same building where the **Declaration of Independence** was signed in 1776. George Washington was chosen to be president of the convention. Benjamin Franklin, James Madison, and Alexander Hamilton were members of the convention, too.

> James Madison's ideas became the basis for the U.S. Constitution. He is often called the "father of the Constitution." He later became the fourth president of the United States.

The Parts of the U.S. Constitution

The U.S. Constitution has three main parts. The first part is called the **preamble**. It begins with the words "we the people," which means it represents all U.S. citizens. This sentence goes on to tell that the Constitution was created "to form a more perfect union," or make a better country.

The second part of the U.S. Constitution contains the articles. An article is a part of a long piece of writing. The articles clearly state that the Constitution is the highest law in the United States. All state constitutions and laws must agree with the U.S. Constitution.

The articles also explain the three branches of government headed by Congress, the president, and the **Supreme Court**. They tell how the powers of the government are divided among these branches. The articles also explain how leaders should be elected or chosen.

> *You can see the original U.S. Constitution at the National Archives in Washington, D.C.*

preamble

articles

White House

Capitol

Supreme Court Building

The articles of the Constitution explain how the branches of government share law-making responsibilities. Congress is made up of two "houses," or parts, called the Senate and the **House of Representatives**. Each state elects two senators. The number of representatives a state has depends on the state's population. The houses of Congress work together to write bills, which they vote on before passing them on to the president.

U.S. citizens elect the president to see that laws are carried out. The president has the power to sign a bill into law, or **veto** it and send it back to Congress. The Supreme Court decides if a law agrees with the Constitution.

In August 1787, the preamble and articles of the Constitution were presented to the Constitutional Convention. They were approved on September 17, 1787.

> The president lives and works in the White House. Congress meets in the Capitol. The Supreme Court makes decisions in the Supreme Court Building.

After the convention, the Constitution was sent to Congress and the states to be **ratified**. Some government leaders still had concerns about the **document**. They didn't want the central government to have too much control over its citizens. They worried that the people would have little power. Many agreed to ratify the Constitution only if a third part was added—the Bill of Rights.

The Bill of Rights is a group of ten amendments, or changes, to the Constitution. It's a list of rights the government can never take away from the people. The amendments were ratified and became part of the Constitution on December 15, 1791.

The first Bill of Rights document, shown here, had twelve amendments. Only ten passed.

Congress of the United States

*begun and held at the City of New-York, on
Wednesday the fourth of March, one thousand seven hundred and eighty-nine.*

THE Conventions of a number of the States, having at the time of their adopting the Constitution, expressed a desire, in order to prevent misconstruction or abuse of its powers, that further declaratory and restrictive clauses should be added: And as extending the ground of public confidence in the Government, will best ensure the beneficent ends of its institution.

RESOLVED by the Senate and House of Representatives of the United States of America, in Congress assembled, two thirds of both Houses concurring, that the following Articles be proposed to the Legislatures of the several States, as amendments to the Constitution of the United States, all, or any of which Articles, when ratified by three fourths of the said Legislatures, to be valid to all intents and purposes, as part of the said Constitution; viz.

ARTICLES in addition to, and amendment of the Constitution of the United States of America, proposed by Congress, and ratified by the Legislatures of the several States, pursuant to the fifth Article of the original Constitution.

Article the first: After the first enumeration required by the first Article of the Constitution, there shall be one Representative for every thirty thousand, until the number shall amount to one hundred, after which the proportion shall be so regulated by Congress, that there shall be not less than one hundred Representatives, nor less than one Representative for every forty thousand persons, until the number of Representatives shall amount to two hundred; after which the proportion shall be so regulated by Congress, that there shall not be less than two hundred Representatives, nor more than one Representative for every fifty thousand persons.

Article the second: No law, varying the compensation for the services of the Senators and Representatives, shall take effect, until an election of Representatives shall have intervened.

Article the third: Congress shall make no law respecting an establishment of religion, or prohibiting the free exercise thereof; or abridging the freedom of speech, or of the press; or the right of the people peaceably to assemble, and to petition the Government for a redress of grievances.

Article the fourth: A well regulated militia, being necessary to the security of a free State, the right of the people to keep and bear arms, shall not be infringed.

Article the fifth: No soldier shall, in time of peace be quartered in any house, without the consent of the owner, nor in time of war, but in a manner to be prescribed by law.

Article the sixth: The right of the people to be secure in their persons, houses, papers, and effects, against unreasonable searches and seizures, shall not be violated, and no warrants shall issue, but upon probable cause, supported by oath or affirmation, and particularly describing the place to be searched, and the persons or things to be seized.

Article the seventh: No person shall be held to answer for a capital, or otherwise infamous crime, unless on a presentment or indictment of a Grand Jury, except in cases arising in the land or naval forces, or in the Militia, when in actual service in time of war or public danger; nor shall any person be subject for the same offence to be twice put in jeopardy of life or limb; nor shall be compelled in any criminal case to be a witness against himself, nor be deprived of life, liberty, or property, without due process of law; nor shall private property be taken for public use, without just compensation.

Article the eighth: In all criminal prosecutions, the accused shall enjoy the right to a speedy and public trial, by an impartial jury of the State and district wherein the crime shall have been committed, which district shall have been previously ascertained by law, and to be informed of the nature and cause of the accusation; to be confronted with the witnesses against him; to have compulsory process for obtaining witnesses in his favor, and to have the assistance of counsel for his defence.

Article the ninth: In suits at common law, where the value in controversy shall exceed twenty dollars, the right of trial by jury shall be preserved, and no fact tried by a jury, shall be otherwise re-examined in any court of the United States, than according to the rules of the common law.

Article the tenth: Excessive bail shall not be required, nor excessive fines imposed, nor cruel and unusual punishments inflicted.

Article the eleventh: The enumeration in the Constitution, of certain rights, shall not be construed to deny or disparage others retained by the people.

Article the twelfth: The powers not delegated to the United States by the Constitution, nor prohibited by it to the States, are reserved to the States respectively, or to the people.

ATTEST,

Frederick Augustus Muhlenberg, Speaker of the House of Representatives.
John Adams, Vice President of the United States, and President of the Senate.

John Beckley, Clerk of the House of Representatives.
Sam. A. Otis, Secretary of the Senate.

Parts of the U.S. Constitution

Bill of Rights
- protects the rights of U.S. citizens
- limits the power of the government

preamble
- explains why the Constitution was written

other amendments
- changes and additions to the Constitution

articles
- explain how the government works

The Bill of Rights

The Bill of Rights gives U.S. citizens freedom in several ways. For example, the First Amendment promises freedom of speech. This means that you can speak and write your views. In some countries, a person can be jailed for speaking against the government. Other amendments promise that a person who is blamed for a crime gets a trial by jury and the same rights as everyone else. The Tenth Amendment says that powers not listed as belonging to the central government belong to the states.

Over time, more amendments were added to the Constitution as the country changed. In 1865, the Thirteenth Amendment made slavery illegal. The Twenty-seventh Amendment, which dealt with salaries in Congress, was added in 1992. More amendments may be added in the future.

Women fought for the right to vote for years. In 1920, the Nineteenth Amendment promised them this right.

Why Do We Have Constitution Day?

As years passed, some people began to worry that U.S. citizens, especially children, didn't know enough about their country and its constitution. Several people suggested a day to honor citizenship. In 1952, President Harry Truman named the day that the Constitutional Convention approved the Constitution, September 17, as Citizenship Day.

In 2004, Senator Robert Byrd of West Virginia suggested a holiday for schools to honor the Constitution. Congress and the president made his idea into law by changing Citizenship Day to Constitution Day. All schools that receive money from the government must set aside time on this day to teach about the Constitution. If September 17 falls on a weekend, Constitution Day is observed on the closest weekday.

Robert Byrd studied the Constitution carefully. He wanted all U.S. citizens to understand and value the document that built a nation.

Harry Truman

Robert Byrd

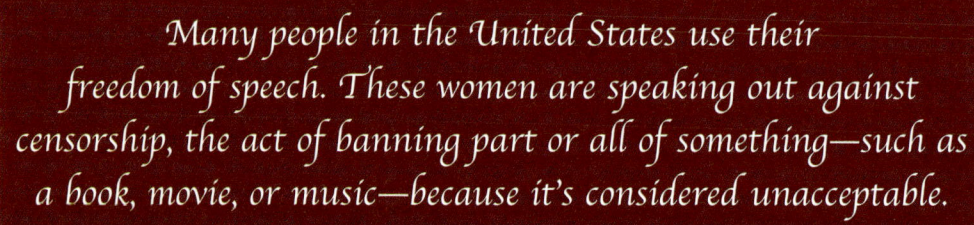

Many people in the United States use their freedom of speech. These women are speaking out against censorship, the act of banning part or all of something—such as a book, movie, or music—because it's considered unacceptable.

Ways to Celebrate Constitution Day

You can celebrate Constitution Day by learning about the Constitution. Here are a few ideas for a group of students:

- Act out the Constitutional Convention with your class or school. Students can be chosen to represent states at the convention.

- Plan a Constitution Day fair at your school. Students can study a small part of the document.

- Study an amendment in the Bill of Rights. Find out if people today have different views about what this amendment means. Plan a **debate** between two people or groups with different opinions.

- Write an idea for a new amendment. Your class can act as Congress. Ask "Congress" to vote for your amendment. Have your teacher act as president.

- Create a Web site to teach others more about the Constitution.

Reading the Constitution may seem hard at first, but books and Web sites can help you. Here are more ways to study the Constitution by yourself:

- Make a board game that provides questions and answers based on the Constitution.

- Compare the U.S. Constitution to another country's constitution. Make a chart showing how they're alike and different.

- Compare your state constitution to the U.S. Constitution. Make a chart describing each document and how powers are divided or shared.

- Write a constitution for your school or neighborhood using the Constitution as a guide.

The more you learn about the U.S. Constitution, the more you'll value it. Although Constitution Day is only once a year, we should honor this document all year long.

The library is a great place to study and find books about the U.S. Constitution.

The U.S. Constitution
From Convention to Holiday

- **May 1787** – Constitutional Convention meets

- **September 1787** – Constitutional Convention approves U.S. Constitution

- **June 1788** – New Hampshire is the ninth state to ratify the Constitution, making it official

- **December 1791** – Bill of Rights is added to the Constitution

- **December 1865** – Thirteenth Amendment frees slaves

- **August 1920** – Nineteenth Amendment gives women the right to vote

- **February 1952** – Citizenship Day becomes a holiday

- **December 2004** – Citizenship Day changes to Constitution Day

Glossary

Articles of Confederation (AHR-tih-kuhlz UV kuhn-feh-duh-RAY-shun) The plan for the national government of the United States before the Constitution was created.

celebrate (SEH-luh-brayt) To do actions on a day to honor someone or something.

constitution (kahn-stuh-TOO-shun) A written document that tells the basic way a government is set up.

convention (kuhn-VEHN-shuhn) When a group of people gathers to form a plan.

debate (dih-BAYT) A meeting at which people or groups argue points of view.

Declaration of Independence (deh-kluh-RAY-shun UV ihn-duh-PEHN-duhns) An announcement signed on July 4, 1776, in which American colonists stated they were free of British rule.

document (DAH-kyoo-muhnt) A written paper.

House of Representatives (HOWS UV reh-prih-ZEHN-tuh-tihvz) A part of Congress, which is the law-making body of the U.S. government.

preamble (pree-AM-buhl) A beginning of a document that explains what follows.

ratify (RAA-tuh-fy) To agree to or approve something.

Supreme Court (suh-PREEM KORT) The highest court in the United States.

veto (VEE-toh) To refuse to sign a bill from Congress and keep it from becoming a law.

Index

A
amendment(s), 12, 14, 15, 19
article(s), 8, 11, 14
Articles of Confederation, 7

B
Bill of Rights, 12, 14, 15, 19, 22
branches of government, 8, 11
Byrd, Senator Robert, 16

C
Citizenship Day, 16, 22
Congress, 8, 11, 12, 15, 16, 19
Constitutional Convention, 7, 11, 16, 19, 22

D
Declaration of Independence, 7

F
First Amendment, 15
Franklin, Benjamin, 7

H
Hamilton, Alexander, 7
House of Representatives, 11

M
Madison, James, 7

N
New Hampshire, 22
Nineteenth Amendment, 22

P
Philadelphia, Pennsylvania, 7
preamble, 8, 11, 14
president, 8, 11, 19

R
ratify(ied), 12, 22

S
Senate, 11
Supreme Court, 8, 11

T
Tenth Amendment, 15
Thirteenth Amendment, 15, 22
Truman, President Harry, 16
Twenty-seventh Amendment, 15

V
veto, 11

W
Washington, George, 7

Due to the changing nature of Internet links, The Rosen Publishing Group, Inc., has developed an online list of Web sites related to the subject of this book. This site is updated regularly. Please use this link to access the list: http://www.rcbmlinks.com/rlr/cday